CANADA
the people

Bobbie Kalman

The Lands, Peoples, and Cultures Series

Toronto · Oxford · New York
Crabtree Publishing Company

The Lands, Peoples, and Cultures Series
Created by Bobbie Kalman

For Malin Akerman

Editor-in-chief
Bobbie Kalman

Writing team
Bobbie Kalman
Janine Schaub
David Schimpky
Lynda Hale

Editors
David Schimpky
Lynda Hale
Tammy Everts

Research
Janine Schaub

Design and computer layout
Antoinette "Cookie" DeBiasi

Cover mechanicals
Rose Campbell

Illustrations
Antoinette "Cookie" DeBiasi

Printer
Worzalla Publishing Company

Separations and film
Kedia Inc.

Special thanks to: Canadian International Development Agency; Anne and Lauren Brooks; The Charlottetown Festival; Tourism Saskatchewan; Confederation Life Group of Companies; Terry Fox Foundation; Betty Fox; St. Catharines Historical Museum; Industry, Science, and Technology Canada; Health and Welfare Canada; National Archives of Canada; the librarians and students of Michael J. Brennan and Pine Grove Elementary Schools: Maria Picard, Bill McBride, Stacey Baugaard, Kelly Joshua, Connor O'Sullivan, Jason Chan, Craig Prince, Shantelle Bascus, and Jeri-Lynn Webster

Photographs

CIDA photo/Dilip Mekta: page 25 (top)
CIDA photo/Roger Lemoyne: page 25 (bottom)
Charlottetown Festival production/ Anne of Green Gables: page 5 (bottom)
Confederation Life Gallery of Canadian History: pages 9, 29
Canapress Photo Service: page 30 (right)
Marc Crabtree: pages 10, 11 (left), 13, 14, 16 (top), 17, 18, 19 (bottom left), 20 (right), 24
Industry, Science, and Technology Canada: pages 3, 5 (top left, middle left and right), 6 (bottom), 20 (top), 21 (top left, right, and bottom), 22 (top left), 23 (top)
Terry Fox Foundation: page 30 (left)

Health and Welfare Canada: page 16 (bottom)
Health and Welfare/Tessa Macintosh: page 19 (bottom right)
James Kamstra: pages 4, 22 (right), 26-27
Bobbie Kalman: pages 5 (top right), 19 (top), 21 (middle), 22 (bottom left)
Diane Payton Majumdar: title page, pages 4 (border), 11 (right)
National Archives of Canada/C-1118: page 8
Peter Peroff: page 15
St. Catharines Historical Museum: page 12 (top)
Janine Schaub: page 23 (bottom left)
Tourism Saskatchewan: cover, pages 6 (top), 7, 20 (left), 23 (circle)
André Baude: page 23 (bottom right)

Published by
Crabtree Publishing Company

350 Fifth Avenue	360 York Road, RR 4,	73 Lime Walk
Suite 3308	Niagara-on-the-Lake,	Headington
New York	Ontario, Canada	Oxford OX3 7AD
N.Y. 10118	L0S 1J0	United Kingdom

Cataloguing in Publication Data

Kalman, Bobbie, 1947-
  Canada: the people

(Lands, Peoples, and Cultures Series)
Includes index.
ISBN 0-86505-218-2 (library bound) ISBN 0-86505-298-0 (pbk.)
The heritage of Canada's various peoples, along with the everyday lives of Canadians, are among the topics discussed in this book.

1. Canada - Social conditions - Juvenile literature.
I. Title. II. Series.

HB103.5.K35 1993   j971   LC 93-34328

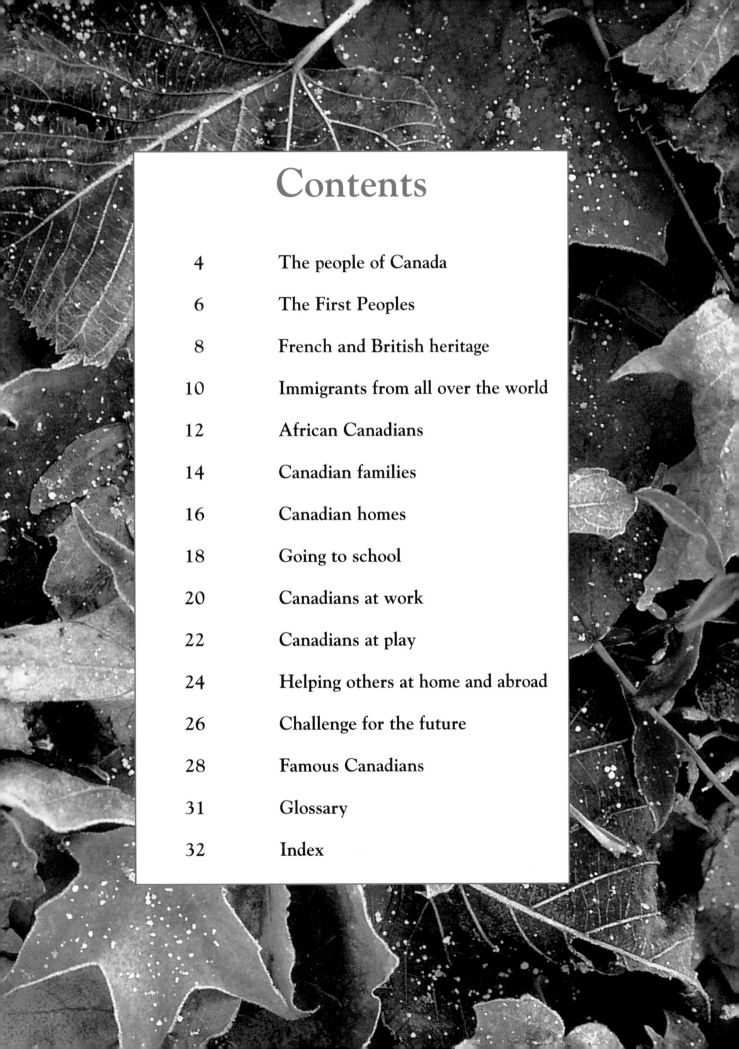

Contents

 The people of Canada

Imagine Canada as a huge patchwork quilt. Framed by the Atlantic Ocean on the east coast, the Pacific Ocean on the west, the Arctic Ocean to the north, and the United States border to the south, the background of the quilt is a blend of mountains, plains, rivers, and lakes. The many faces of Canada's people are the exciting designs on each patch.

People from every corner of the world have immigrated to Canada. Their cultures and languages add colorful variety to the giant quilt. This mixture of nationalities is called **multiculturalism**, which means "many cultures." Canadians celebrate and respect one another's heritage.

Canadian personalities

People who try to describe the "Canadian character" find it difficult because of the cultural variety and different ways of life in Canada. Since words cannot describe the Canadian personality, perhaps these pictures will help capture the Canadian spirit.

Canadians set high goals and work as a team to accomplish them!

Canadians are scientific and industrious.

Canadians love to have fun.

(left) Canadians are proud of their heritage.
(below) Canadians are creative and talented.

(right) Canadians are adventurous.

The First Peoples

People have lived in the area that is now Canada for thousands of years. Some scientists say the first Native peoples traveled to North America from Asia across a strip of land that once joined the two continents. Others argue that they came from South America and have lived on this continent for more than 40,000 years!

Community life

The societies of Native peoples were very organized. Each person had a special role but, at the same time, everyone worked together for the good of the community. Some groups moved from place to place, following the herds of animals they hunted for food. Others lived in villages along the shores of Canada's many waterways. They used spears, nets, and hooks to catch the plentiful fish for their food. There were also tribes that farmed the land. They settled in one place and grew vegetables such as corn, beans, and squash.

Native nations

Today many different Native groups live in Canada, each with its own traditions and language. Eastern Canada is home to the Maliseet, Algonquin, Iroquois, Micmac, Huron, and Ojibwa. Native nations of the plains include the Blackfoot, Cree, and Assiniboine. Kwakiutl, Bella Coola, and Haida communities can be found on the Pacific coast. The Dene, Tsimshian, and Slavey peoples live in the subarctic regions. These groups and many more are the descendants of the First Peoples of North America.

The Métis

During fur-trading days, French traders married into Native tribes. Their descendants, the Métis, are of mixed Native and French origins. Most live in Manitoba and Alberta. Their religion is Catholic, but Native customs and beliefs have been added. Their language combines Cree, French and English words. The Métis celebrate with a combination of French-Canadian jigs and Native dances.

The people of the north

One group of Native people chose the harsh northern part of the world, called the Arctic, as their home. They are the Inuit, which means "the people." Their ancestors migrated from Asia to the extreme climate of Canada's Arctic about 4000 years ago, much later than other Native groups. Until recently they were **nomadic** hunters, traveling across the north in search of food. Inuit culture is based on knowledge of the land, sea, and animals. The Inuit still use centuries-old hunting techniques.

New Native pride

Although the modern world has destroyed much of their traditional culture, the Native peoples of Canada are rediscovering their heritage. Learning old skills, dances, songs, and games has renewed Native cultural pride. To remember their heritage, Native groups get together for celebrations such as the powwow.

Taking back the land

In 1999 the map of Canada will show a new northern territory called **Nunavut**. This region, which is now a part of the Northwest Territories, will be governed by the Inuit. The creation of Nunavut is part of an effort to give homelands back to the Native peoples of Canada. The Dene, who also live in the north, hope to have a homeland called **Denedeh** in the near future. The Native peoples living in other parts of Canada are also asking the government to return the lands that had been taken wrongfully from their ancestors.

(opposite page top) These children are all dressed up for a powwow celebration in Saskatchewan.
(opposite bottom) The Inuit live in the Arctic.
(below) The lives of Native peoples changed when Europeans came to Canada. Today, Native leaders are fighting to regain the land that was taken from them.

🗿 French and British heritage 🗿

The first Europeans to settle and remain in Canada were the French. In 1605 an explorer named Samuel de Champlain started a small settlement called Port Royal in what is now Nova Scotia. The cold winters of Canada were a big shock to the settlers who were used to the much milder climate of France. Most of the Port Royal settlers returned to France by 1607. In 1608 Champlain started another French settlement called "The Habitation" on the shores of the St. Lawrence River. Despite many difficulties, this settlement was a success. Today it is known as Quebec City, the capital of the province of Quebec.

The habitants

To encourage French settlers to leave France and live in the Canadian colonies, the French king offered large areas of free farmland to privileged people who became *seigneurs*, or lords. The seigneurs brought experienced farmers from France to work on their land. These farmers were called *habitants*. The habitants cleared the land of trees and stones and planted fields that yielded plentiful crops. Some took up fur trading. The colony's population increased rapidly because the habitants raised large families.

French Canada today

Today 27 percent of Canada's population is of French heritage. Although most live in Quebec, many French Canadians make their home in Ontario, New Brunswick, and Manitoba. French Canadians are proud of their heritage. Many of their traditions and customs date back to habitant days. On every Quebec license plate, the phrase "Je me souviens," which means "I remember," reminds French Canadians of their history in Canada.

French-Canadian culture is as strong today as it was 100 years ago.

Thousand of Loyalists came to Canada because of the American Revolution.

The United Empire Loyalists

More than two-thirds of Canada's citizens are English-speaking, and 40 percent are of British descent. The largest group of British immigrants came to Canada from the Thirteen Colonies between the years 1775 and 1791. During this time, the American colonists were fighting for their independence from Britain. Some colonists, however, remained loyal to their mother country and were known as **United Empire Loyalists**. They moved north into the territories that were still held by Britain. The Loyalists were given plots of land in areas that are now the provinces of Prince Edward Island, New Brunswick, Nova Scotia, Ontario, and Quebec.

Soon after the Loyalists settled in Canada, more immigrants from England, Scotland, and Ireland arrived. Today, much of Canada's culture reflects its British roots. The language, traditions, and holidays of this country are similar to those of Great Britain, the United States, and Australia.

Bilingual Canada

Since English and French are the two main languages spoken in Canada, the government has declared Canada a **bilingual** country. Bilingual simply means "having two languages." Bilingualism affects many aspects of Canadian life. Students learn both French and English in school. Wherever Canadians live or travel in Canada, they can receive important government services in two languages. Every product sold in Canada must have both French and English information on its label. For example, a can of beans has "green beans" written on one side and "haricots verts" on the other.

Not all Canadians believe that bilingualism is a good idea. Some English Canadians feel that it is unnecessary in parts of Canada where French is rarely spoken. On the other hand, many people who live in Quebec claim that the presence of the English language in their province threatens the survival of the French language.

Immigrants from all over the world

In 1868 the government of Canada bought a huge area of land called Rupert's Land from the Hudson's Bay Company. The Hudson's Bay Company had used Rupert's Land for fur trading since 1670. The new Canadian territory stretched from the western border of Ontario to British Columbia. By 1885, a railway was built across Canada, allowing people to travel to the west and settle the new lands.

The settlers of the west

Canada wanted people to farm the western lands, even though several Native nations lived in this region. The future of the Native peoples was not considered in Canada's plans. The government advertised cheap plots of farmland in the "last best west" to people in the eastern part of Canada and to those who lived in the United States and Britain.

The advertisements were meant to attract English-speaking farmers of European descent, but only a few came to the west. In 1896 the Canadian government began advertising land to non-English-speaking Europeans as well. Thousands of Russians, Rumanians, Belgians, Austrians, Scandinavians, Mennonites, Ukrainians, and other European settlers flocked to western Canada. They established farms across the prairies. The prairie provinces still celebrate their European heritages with many festivals throughout the year.

Every culture under the sun

For a long time, Canada closed its doors to people who did not have a European background. In recent years, however, it has welcomed immigrants from Asia, the Caribbean, South America, and Africa. Some were refugees, fleeing from hunger and war in their home countries. Others came for the opportunity to live in a wealthier land. The largest group of recent immigrants is from the Far East. Thousands of Chinese from Hong Kong have immigrated to Canada because their city will soon become part of communist China. Most settle in large cities such as Toronto and Vancouver.

Where people live

When new Canadians first come into the country, many choose to live in the big cities. As good job opportunities or better living conditions become available, some of them move to other areas. As a result, people of different cultural backgrounds can be found all over Canada.

(opposite page) A Muslim girl in Vancouver
(below) Most Chinese immigrants live in big cities.

African Canadians

African Canadians have lived in Canada for almost 400 years. The first were taken from Africa to work as slaves in French-Canadian households. Hundreds more came to Canada with the Loyalists. Some were slaves of wealthy families; others were free men and women who were loyal to Britain. In 1834 a law made slavery illegal in Canada. African Canadians did not enjoy the same advantages as those enjoyed by Canadians of European descent, but they were happy to be free.

The Underground Railroad

"Freedom can be found if you follow the North Star to Canada" was a popular phrase among American slaves. Some slaves may have found freedom by following a star, but most followed the Underground Railroad to Canada. Despite its name, there were no trains on the Underground Railroad, and it was not underground.

The Underground Railroad was a network of people who helped slaves escape from the American South. Railway terms were used as a code for the activities of its helpers. For example, a house or barn that was a safe place to stop for the night was a **station**, and a person who acted as a guide was a **conductor**. Slaves were smuggled from safe house to safe house until they reached freedom in Canada. Canadians who opposed slavery, called **abolitionists**, helped the refugees find jobs. They raised money to feed, clothe, and house the new Canadians until they could support themselves.

The Canadian connection

Harriet Tubman, a famous African-American abolitionist, lived in Canada for several years. A courageous and intelligent woman, she was one of the most active conductors on the Underground Railroad. She used St. Catharines, Ontario, as her base and helped as many as 300 slaves find freedom in Canada.

An inspiration

Josiah Henson was born a slave in Kentucky in 1789. With the help of the Underground Railroad, he and his family escaped to Canada. He became a Methodist minister and provided help to ex-slaves who had recently arrived from the United States. Henson set up a school in Dresden, Ontario, to train runaway slaves for jobs. Many people believe that parts of his life were the inspiration for *Uncle Tom's Cabin*, a famous novel written by American author Harriet Beecher Stowe.

Against the odds

Mary Shadd Cary was raised in the northern United States and moved to Canada at the age of 28. In the town of Windsor, Ontario, she became editor of a newspaper called the *Provincial Freeman*. Cary was the first black woman in North America to edit a newspaper. During this time in history, it was difficult for women to have successful careers, and it was even more difficult for a woman of African descent. Against all odds, Mary Shadd Cary became a great success!

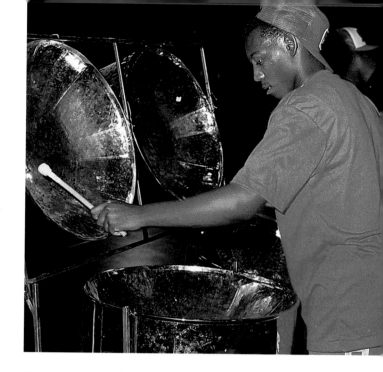

Living in the cities

During the Great Depression of the 1930s, many African-Canadian farmers moved to the cities to find jobs. Over the last thirty years, more than a half million people of African origin have immigrated to Canada from the United States, Africa, and the Caribbean. Most have chosen to settle in cities. Many Canadian cities have centers where African-Canadians can meet and share their culture.

Fighting prejudice

Unfortunately, some African Canadians are victims of **racism**. Racism is the belief that one race is superior to another. Most Canadians want a country in which all people can live together in harmony, and they believe that education is the most powerful way to stop racist attitudes. Schools have programs that encourage children to appreciate the different races and cultures in Canada. Police forces and government agencies are hiring employees who represent the many faces of Canada's multicultural society.

(opposite page top) Harriet Tubman helped many slaves reach safety in Canada. (opposite page bottom) Thousands of slaves found freedom with the help of the Underground Railroad. (above) African Canadians share their music and culture in festivals such as Caribana, which takes place in Toronto.

 Canadian families

Some people compare a family to the foundation of a building. If the foundation is strong, the building will be strong. In the same way, families are important in building a strong country. Families have changed a lot in the last fifty years, but they are as important as ever!

Variety in today's family

Families come in all sizes and combinations. Many families are made up of two parents and one to three children. Sometimes couples divorce, and the children are raised by one parent. Another family situation may include a mother and father with children from previous marriages. Some couples live together and raise families, but they do not get married.

Different lifestyles

In the past, fathers went to work outside the home and mothers looked after the house and children. Family members have different roles today. Mothers also work outside the home, and both parents share household duties. Women now have careers that were once held only by men. Many Canadian doctors, scientists, ministers, business executives, and soldiers are women.

The lives of Canadian children have changed, too. When both parents work, arrangements must be made for the care of the children. Many parents send their children to daycare centers or hire live-in nannies to look after them at home. Computers have allowed some parents to do their office work at home so they can be near their children.

The extended family

Grandparents, uncles, aunts, and cousins are called **extended family**. In the past, extended family members lived together or near one another. Today they are spread out across town or across the country. Some even live on opposite sides of the world.

Native families

Native societies are based on families that belong to **clans**, or groups of related members. Younger family members care for the older generation. The **elders** are the senior members who are respected for their knowledge and understanding of traditional ways and teachings. They pass on the ancient knowledge, skills, and values to the young.

Family reunions

Many families have large get-togethers called **reunions**. All family members, including aunts, uncles, and cousins, are invited. Sometimes relatives come from all over the world to reunite with their family.

One example of a big family reunion is the International Gathering of the Clans. It is an annual celebration that brings together Scottish families from all over the world. Scottish clans are determined by the family name, such as MacPherson clan, Ross clan, and Campbell clan. The province of Nova Scotia is often the host of this event because many of its people have Scottish roots.

Strong roots

Family history is very important to Canadians. Some families keep a record called a **family tree**. This diagram, which looks like a tree, shows the names of relatives and how they are related to one another. Does your family have a family tree?

Foster families and adoption

When parents can not care for their children for a certain period of time, other families or couples provide temporary care and support for these **foster** children. Parents who are permanently unable to care for a child may give up that child for **adoption**. Many adopted Canadian children live happy lives with their new families. Some young adults who were adopted when they were children search for their birth parents.

(opposite page) Traditional families have two parents and between one and three children.
(below) Canadians do not always have traditional families or marriages! At this wedding, the couple and wedding party wore costumes. The children from the husband's first marriage took part in the ceremony. A year later, a baby sister became part of this new family.

Canadian homes

Today most Canadians enjoy comfortable lives. They live in well-built houses or apartments equipped with clean, running water, sewers, electricity, television, and telephone services. Their homes are heated in winter, and many are air-conditioned in summer.

Homes usually include bedrooms, bathrooms, a kitchen, a dining area, and a family room. The family room is the center of the home, where parents and children watch television, play games, read books, or just talk with one another.

Country life

Most people who live in small towns or in the country enjoy the luxury of space. Rural Canadians often have single-family homes with a front and back yard. Some live on farms with large areas of land around their homes.

City dwellers

Although there are large homes in big cities, many people live in small houses, apartments, or townhouses. People who live in big cities usually have less space compared to those who live in rural areas. Neighbors may be close and, often, many people live in one dwelling. Tall apartment buildings are home to hundreds of families. The local park serves as the back yard.

(top) Hundreds of people live in one city apartment building. (below) Some arctic homes look like the igloos in which the Inuit once lived.

Life in the suburbs

People who enjoy the benefits of living in a city but want extra space may choose to live in the **suburbs**. Suburbs are communities that have spread out around a city. They consist of single-family homes, townhouses, and apartment buildings that are less crowded than those found in the city. Many of the people who live in the suburbs travel to the nearby city to work or attend school. The suburbs of Toronto, Canada's largest city, are as far as 50 kilometers (30 miles) from the city's center.

All shapes and sizes

Some Canadian homes reflect the culture of their owners. Greek-style homes have large pillars and blue trim, German homes often have balconies decorated with beautiful flowers, and homes in Quebec are influenced by French architecture. Some Inuit homes are dome-shaped, like igloos. Traditional beliefs can also play an important role in the design of a house. A Chinese family, for example, might not build a house with a staircase facing the front door. According to tradition, all the good luck will escape out the door!

Cottage country

Canadians take advantage of Canada's beautiful scenery by owning or renting a **cottage** or **camp**. This country house is a one- to three-hour drive from home. Cottages can be simple cabins located near rivers and lakes or larger homes that can also be used in winter.

Granville Island, which is part of the city of Vancouver, has found one solution to crowded city conditions. Some of its residents have built houses right on the water! The community is called Sea Village. In most ways, Sea Village is like other areas of the city. The residents pay taxes and receive the city's electricity and telephone services. Shopping is just a short trip away—by boat!

Going to school

Children begin their education in elementary school. Their first year is called kindergarten. At some schools, children can start a year earlier with a program called junior kindergarten. After kindergarten, students attend eight grades of elementary school. They study traditional subjects such as math, science, reading, and social studies. They also learn about computers, perform plays, and take field trips to museums and historic sites.

High school
After the eighth grade, students go on to high school, where they can choose many of the subjects they want to study. They take classes that will prepare them for university, community college, or a job. School clubs, concerts, team sports, and dances make secondary school more fun. Some schools offer students special classes in music, ballet, or theater. Of course, the students still have to study regular academic subjects.

Different kinds of schools
There are other kinds of schools in Canada. Separate schools are attended by children from Roman-Catholic families. Private schools advertise higher teaching standards, smaller

classes, and special-interest programs. Public schools and separate schools are paid by taxes. Parents who send their children to private schools, however, must pay a large fee.

One type of private school is called the Montessori school. Montessori schools have small classes, and children of different ages study in the same room. Students are encouraged to learn independently and develop at their own rate with the teacher as their guide and older classmates as role models.

Education for Native peoples
Native children who live in isolated communities go to schools that are operated by the federal government. In the past, these schools taught the children in English or French and tried to force them to forget their Native heritage. Students were sent away to live in larger communities where they felt alone, far from their family and friends.

Today many Native children are educated within their own communities. In addition to regular classes, they learn the language of their ancestors and traditional skills such as hunting and making crafts. Some modern Native schools also provide showers and hot meals.

Universities and colleges
Young Canadians who wish to continue their education can choose to go to community college or university. Community colleges train students for special types of jobs, such as computer programming, fashion design, plumbing, and photography. Universities teach students how to gain knowledge in many fields of study. Teachers, doctors, lawyers, and dentists go to university to be trained in their professions.

(left) The National Ballet School of Canada is a unique private school. Students take classes such as math, science, English, and history but also receive many hours of ballet instruction.

(top) Performing arts high schools, such as Niagara District Secondary School, provide students with the theater skills of singing, dancing, script writing, and directing. The students also take regular subjects.
(left) At this school, Canadian Muslim children learn to read in English as well as in their heritage language.
(above) Some Native schools train students in such skills as hunting and working with hides. Traditional languages and beliefs are taught in addition to subjects learned by students in other schools.

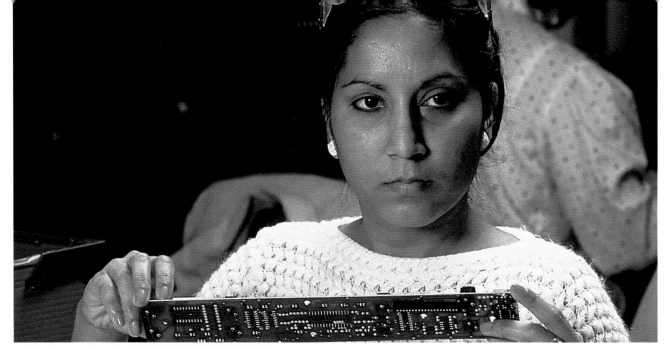

Canadians at work

Canadians work at a variety of occupations. Some hold jobs in accounting, engineering, medicine, or law. Others work in factories, making the products that we use every day. Many Canadians own businesses, which can range from a corner store to a huge corporation. Young Canadians have many choices when they leave school. Which careers interest you?

(top) Canadians hold a variety of jobs. Some work in the high-tech industry. (left) Being a Mountie is a truly Canadian occupation. (above) Women, such as this doctor, are now in professions once held only by men.

(above) Some Canadians work in factories.
(oval) Fishing is the occupation of many Canadians who live in the Atlantic provinces.
(right) Many families make their living by running a family business, such as this grocery store.
(below) The majority of Canadians work in the service industry. The service industry provides jobs for bankers, accountants, store clerks, lawyers, hair stylists, taxi drivers, and all kinds of office workers.

Watching television, reading, making crafts, listening to music, playing games, and visiting friends are some ways in which Canadians spend their leisure time. The cold winters, warm summers, and beautiful landscapes of Canada make it possible for people to enjoy many outdoor activities.

Popular winter sports

Exciting winter sports make the long, cold Canadian winter a season of fun! A sport that is well suited to Canada's mountains and forests is skiing. Downhill skiers take a lift to the top of a mountain and then glide down at great speeds. Cross-country skiers prefer to travel at a slower pace on a forest trail. Some Canadians enjoy the thrill of snowmobiling. Skating and hockey are other favorite Canadian winter sports. Skating rinks can be found in every town and city.

On the move

Canadians love to travel! University students often backpack around the world before they begin their careers. Young couples fly to Europe to explore historic sites and experience different ways of life. Florida, Mexico, and the Caribbean islands are favorite destinations of families looking for a warm vacation to escape the cold winter. Closer to home, Canadians of all ages visit cities such as Vancouver, Toronto, and Quebec City for exciting adventures in theater, shopping, and sightseeing. Some Canadian travelers prefer the peace and beauty of the Canadian wilderness. They enjoy camping trips in Canada's many parks.

(left) Skiing makes winter much more enjoyable.
(circle) Visiting with grandparents is a happy way to spend an afternoon.
(below) I caught a big one!

(top) Canoes and kayaks, which were invented by the Native peoples, are still popular ways to explore the wilderness areas of Canada.

(below) Hockey is one of Canada's favorite games. Canadian children are never too young to learn this thrilling sport!

(circle) Listening to music is very relaxing.

(below right) Young people today are traveling all over the world. Samantha visited Paris on an exchange program.

Helping others at home and abroad

Canadians pride themselves on being caring people. Canada's social programs reflect that attitude. The government collects taxes from working Canadians and those who own property. This money is used for a variety of services from which all Canadians can benefit if they need help. Some tax money is used to aid people in other countries.

Health insurance

When Canadians are sick or injured, most of their medical bills are paid by provincial health insurance, even if they are in the hospital for a long time. The health-care system guarantees that Canadians receive treatment according to their needs and not their ability to pay.

Family aid and pensions

Some families have difficulty making ends meet. Fortunately, they can receive help from the government in the form of a monthly allowance. When people grow older, they also receive aid. Everyone over the age of 65 receives a regular government payment called a **pension**.

Unemployment insurance

The Canadian Unemployment Insurance program is a safety net for working people. If they lose their job, they can continue to receive a part of their former salary from the government for a period of time. This insurance allows unemployed workers to pay their bills until they find new jobs.

Helping other countries

Canada has a worldwide reputation for sending aid to less-developed nations. Aid is given through the Canadian International Development Agency (CIDA). CIDA distributes food to famine victims, sends medical supplies to disaster zones, teaches farmers modern agricultural techniques, and helps build factories and wells.

Peacekeeping

Canada's armed forces often participate in United Nations (UN) peacekeeping operations. The UN sends soldiers from many different countries to help enforce peace agreements and prevent violence. Former Canadian Prime Minister Lester B. Pearson was awarded the Nobel Peace Prize for creating the first UN peacekeeping force in 1957. He was Canada's ambassador to the UN at the time. Canadians are proud of their country's involvement in UN activities in the Persian Gulf, Cyprus, Somalia, and Bosnia-Hercegovina.

Help through the community

Many Canadians provide further help for people in Canada and around the world. Community organizations, churches, and cultural groups help raise money to send food and medical aid to nations who need assistance. Other Canadian groups operate food banks, which distribute food to people who cannot afford to buy groceries. Some groups shelter the homeless and offer counseling to alcoholics and drug addicts.

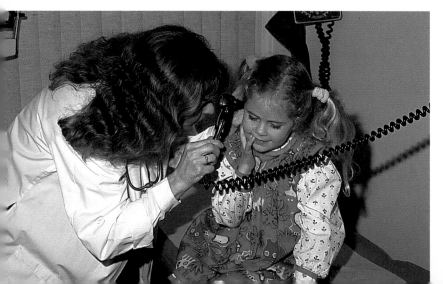

(left) All Canadians are entitled to quality health care throughout the country.
(opposite page) The Canadian International Development Agency teaches new skills to people in less-developed nations. This organization also gives aid to famine victims around the world. Canada contributes over two billion dollars each year to help other countries.

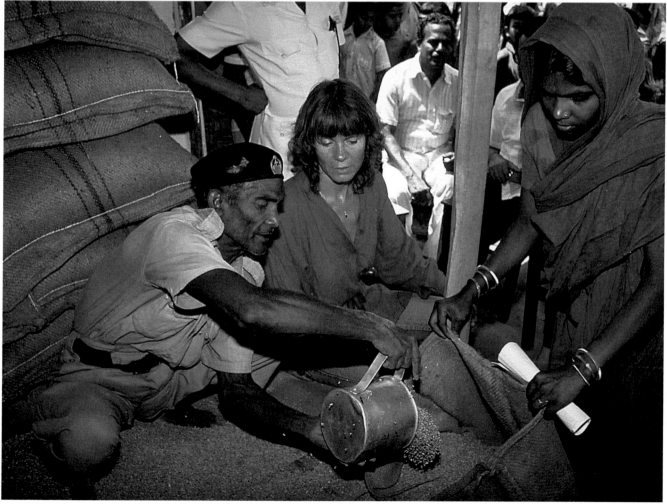

Challenge for the future

Canada's future depends on overcoming several challenges. These problems are not new; their roots go far back in history. Canadians must work hard if they are to correct the mistakes of the past and move on to a better future.

The treatment of Native peoples

Native peoples have experienced much injustice at the hands of non-Native Canadians. In the past, people of European descent tried to stamp out the various Native cultures. Many nations had their lands taken from them by the government. They were forced to live on **reserves** in isolated parts of the country.

Today, the Native peoples who live on reserves are assisted by the federal government of Canada. Even with the help of the government,

however, life is difficult. Native homes often lack running water and flush toilets. Sometimes as many as 20 people must live in one two-room house! Problems such as unemployment, family violence, poor health conditions, drug abuse, and suicide are common.

Working on solutions

Native groups, together with the federal government, are working hard to improve life for Native peoples. Many reserves are now governed by traditional leaders, such as a chief or a council of elders. To meet special needs, some reserves have Native police and counseling services. Several reserves now offer health-care treatment based on traditional healing methods. Despite these efforts, there is still much to be accomplished.

French and English relations

Another challenge facing the future of Canada is that of French-English relations. Some French-speaking people in Quebec want to separate from Canada and form their own country. Other Canadians, however, believe that Quebec is an important part of Canada and do not wish to see the country split apart.

The Constitution Act

A **constitution** is the law that governs a country. For many years, Canada did not have its own constitution. The law that governed Canada was an act of British Parliament called the British North America Act. In 1982 former Canadian Prime Minister Pierre Trudeau negotiated an agreement with all the provinces except Quebec. This agreement made Canada's constitution an act of Canadian Parliament. A few changes, such as making the country bilingual and adding some rights for Native peoples, were written into the Constitution Act of 1982. The Constitution Act, however, was far from being a new constitution.

A new constitution?

To meet the needs of Canadians today, the government has made two attempts at developing a new constitution. The Meech Lake and Charlottetown Accords were the names of those proposals. Both failed to win the support of the Canadian people. Some felt that the proposals did not deal properly with the relationship between Quebec and the rest of Canada. Others argued that the interests of Native peoples, women, and other minorities received too little attention. Canadians want a constitution that represents all Canadians, but many wonder if all Canadians will ever agree on what that means!

Famous Canadians

1. *Wayne Gretzky*
2. *Nellie McClung*
3. *Sir Frederick Banting*
4. *Grey Owl*
5. *Norman Bethune*

A champion for women

Until 1917, Canadian women did not have the right to vote. A woman named Nellie McClung, who lived in Manitoba, helped change this injustice by writing about it, conducting speaking tours, and staging public protests. She used her marvelous sense of humor to convince her opponents that she was right. Later, McClung was elected a member of the provincial assembly of Alberta, where she continued her fight for women's rights.

Banting and his team

In 1921 a team of four Canadian scientists discovered **insulin**, a substance that controls a disease called **diabetes**. Sir Frederick Banting,

Charles Best, James Collip, and J.R. Macleod discovered and purified insulin in just nine months! Thanks to insulin, people with diabetes can live normal and healthy lives. In 1923 Banting and Macleod were awarded the Nobel Prize in medicine for their important discovery. They shared the prize with the other two members of their team.

The Great One

"The Great One" is the nickname given to Canadian hockey superstar Wayne Gretzky. Gretzky, like many Canadians, learned hockey from his father on a backyard ice rink. As a teenager, he became one of the youngest players in major-league sports. For years Gretzky played with the Edmonton Oilers, breaking more hockey records than any other player in history. Canadians were saddened when he was traded to the Los Angeles Kings in the United States.

The great conservationist

Grey Owl was one of the first Canadians to speak publicly about the importance of preserving nature. Born in England, he moved to Canada and adopted a Native way of life. He married an Iroquois woman named Anahereo, who taught him about the need for conserving wildlife. In 1931 he began writing books about nature and conservation. He worked as a game warden in Canada's national parks, where he ran several beaver-conservation programs and continued his writing. Grey Owl became famous for his beliefs about protecting the environment.

A hero to the Chinese

Norman Bethune was a Canadian doctor who volunteered his medical services during wars in Spain and China. In Spain he operated a blood-transfusion unit at the front lines. In China he ran the world's first mobile medical unit. He saved the lives of many Chinese and, to this day, he is an honored hero in that country. Bethune died of blood poisoning after accidentally cutting himself while he was performing surgery.

The great inventor Bell

Alexander Graham Bell, the famous inventor, moved to Canada from Scotland when he was 23 years old. Although he worked in the United States in his later years, he returned each summer to do research in Baddeck, Nova Scotia. Bell worked on the development of many inventions, including the iron lung and the phonograph. His most famous invention, however, was the telephone. Bell Canada, Canada's largest telephone company, was founded by Alexander Graham Bell.

On August 10, 1876, Alexander Graham Bell made the first long-distance telephone call from a shoe store in Paris, Ontario to the town of Brantford, Ontario.

Marathon of hope

In 1980 Terry Fox undertook a great challenge—to run across Canada on a "Marathon of Hope" in order to raise funds for cancer research. Fox knew firsthand how great the need for cancer research was. At eighteen years of age his right leg was amputated above the knee as a result of bone cancer. It was at this time, and during the treatment that followed, that Fox saw the pain and despair of others with cancer and knew he wanted to do something about it.

He ran an average of 42 kilometers (26 miles) a day with an artificial leg. Fox's run was cut short when it was discovered that the cancer had spread to his lungs. In 1981 the disease claimed his life. Not only did he raise millions of dollars, but he also inspired the annual "Terry Fox Run," which brings in millions more for cancer research.

Canadian in space

Have you ever wanted to travel in space? Roberta Bondar, a Canadian scientist and physician, had that opportunity in 1992. She was selected to be a part of the crew of the space shuttle "Discovery." She is the first Canadian woman astronaut. While in orbit, she conducted experiments to understand how conditions in space affected the human body. Bondar's achievements have made her a Canadian hero.

☙ Glossary ☙

agriculture Farming

ambassador An official representative of a country who lives in another country

architecture The design of a building

Arctic A cold northern area in which trees do not grow because the land is frozen

cancer A disease in which cells increase at an abnormal rate and destroy healthy tissue

colony A territory governed by a distant country

communist Describing a system in which the government owns all property and controls the use of products and labor in a country

conservation Protection from loss, harm, or waste, especially of natural resources

constitution The document that states the laws by which a country is governed

culture The customs, beliefs, and arts of a distinct group of people

diabetes A disease characterized by too much sugar and too little insulin in the blood

divorce The legal ending of a marriage

elder A senior member of a Native group

ethnic Describing a group of people who share a common culture, race, or origin

famine A widespread lack of food

Far East The eastern part of Asia

federal government The central, or main, government of Canada

food bank An organization that receives donations of food and gives it to people who need it

Hudson's Bay Company A fur-trading company that once controlled most of western Canada

immigrant A person who settles in a new country

iron lung A breathing apparatus that was once used to help people with lung problems

less-developed nation A nation that is unable to satisfy the basic needs of its people, such as food, shelter, proper clothing, health care, and education

Métis A group of people who are of mixed Native and French origins

minority A small group of people within a larger group

Native nation A group of Native people, such as the Micmac or Haida

natural gas An odorless, colorless fuel

Nobel prize An international prize awarded for science, literature, and peace

nomadic Describing a person or group that travels from place to place in search of food

parliament The assembly that makes Canada's laws

pension Money received on a regular basis by people who are retired

phonograph An early record player

powwow A Native celebration that includes feasting and dancing

prairie A large level or gently rolling grassland without trees

racism A belief that one's own race is superior to other races

refugee Someone that leaves a home country because of danger

reserve Land set aside by the government for the exclusive use of Native peoples

rural Describing something in the country

subarctic Of or like regions just south of the Arctic Circle

suburb A residential area near a city

tax Money collected by the government that is based on income, property, services, or purchases

Thirteen Colonies The British colonies that banded together to form the United States

tundra A vast treeless plain found in areas with an arctic climate

☺ Index ☺

3 4 5 6 7 8 9 0 Printed in the U.S.A. 2 0 1 9 8 7 6 5 4